THE BEST FAMILY IN THE WORLD!

THE BEST FAMILY IN THE WORLD!

A book about our greatest joy and our credibility!

by Johannes Amritzer

Original version published in Swedish by www.jcharlieson.se with the title Världens bästa familj

Translation: Jens Charlieson
Cover: Simon Tullberg
Design: Stephanie Elvelyck
Illustrations: Gary A. Smith & Julia Knudtzon
Distributed by Signs & Wonders Media in cooperation with Mission SOS
Printed by Raff Printing Inc. (USA) 2014
ISBN: 978-91-981352-1-3

CONTENTS

DEDICATION

I guess the title of this book says something about to whom it is dedicated. My family will always be the best family in the world, because it is *my* family. To me, there is no better family. I have no other. My wife and children will agree; our family is the best. They have no other. We are the best family in the world for each other! Our joy is in our hands. Maria, Alicia, and Adam - I love you.

-Daddy

But…

The book is also dedicated to the team of pastors serving at SOS Church Stockholm and to all our international pastors and leaders. You are Maria's and my best friends, and faithful allies. Your strong marriages and healthy families inspire us to keep building our own happiness. We learn so much from you. We love you deeply and dearly. You are our closest relatives. Without you we would not be ministering today. Without you we would probably have given up by now. But you were always there and because of that we still live happy lives together in Stockholm and on the mission field. Thank you dear friends for always standing by our side. Thank you for letting us share our lives with you. We are rich to have you!

Your intercessors and friends,

Maria and Johannes Amritzer
Leaders, Mission SOS

FOREWORD

Without a doubt, the most significant issue that we ever face in our life is the issue of relationships. When your relational world is working, everything in your life feels right. When your relationships are broken, nothing in your life feels right.

Of course, the most important relationship in our lives is our relationship with God. Everything starts there. When we get right with God, by trusting Jesus Christ to save us, we take a huge leap forward in terms of making every other relationship in our life work better. The Holy Spirit Himself lives with us to guide us in making the proper decisions for a healthy relational life.

But even with the Holy Spirit's help, we need the guidance of the Scriptures and of pastors and leaders in our life that can help us navigate through all challenges of finding the right spouse, dating healthily, living in a vibrant marriage, and in raising children who are champions.

My good friend, Johannes Amritzer, has provided us with a tremendous gift in this book, THE BEST FAMILY IN THE WORLD. Johannes has a way of combining a clear understanding of the Bible with a raw, direct, gut-level perspective of real life situations, problems, and emotions. He not only models what a marriage should look like, in his relationship with Maria, but also what it is to live a sold-out and adventurous life in Christ. He also has personal experience in parenting two tremendous young people in Alicia and Adam and he is able to speak out of his life as well as from his Biblical study.

I have been pastoring at Allison Park Church for almost 23 years now. Over the past few years, I would have to say that the #1 challenge we face in ministry is the challenge of people who navigate through the complications of confusing and painful relationships. In the pages of this book you will find some very clear and compelling advice as to how to make some wise choices in your present and future relationships.

Remember, God is a healing God. He can restore broken hearts and reconcile damaged relationships. As we seek to obey His commands, He releases His grace into our lives. I pray that God will do just that as you study and apply the Biblical lessons in this book.

Jeff Leake
Lead Pastor, Allison Park Church
President, Reach Northeast

FOREWORD BY THE AUTHOR

This book was primarily written as a guide for pre-marriage counseling. Couples who are just about to be married actually need help with more than the seating arrangements at the wedding reception. Getting married is not about hiring the most professional wedding photographer or caterer. No matter how carefully you choose the bride's bouquet or how "hip" and fashionable the wedding dress is, you will still laugh at it 20 years from now. Couples that are about to get married need to understand that they can be really happy without a honeymoon to the Caribbean, but they might not survive their first year under the same roof without proactive Biblical guidance.

Priests, pastors and spiritual leaders can use this book as a tool in preparation for marriage. My humble hope is that we do not keep re-inventing the wheel, but that we instead help one another. Hopefully this book will be an aid for Christian leaders but also for couples who want to gain knowledge on their own on how to build a sound family! Pastors, if you choose to use this book, ask the people you are about to wed to read it carefully. Then talk about what they have read and ask all those questions that only you can and must ask. Do not forget that you have a unique role as their pastor or priest and that the couple has chosen you because they trust you. You are in fact the only person with this kind of authority over their lives, so therefore, be very straightforward and blunt and do your job thoroughly.

What you are holding in your hands is simply a summary of my notes from some 50 pre-marriage counseling sessions held over the 20+ years that I have had the privilege of wedding people. The book is also a condensed version of all the seminars that I have held on this theme during my years as a local pastor.

This little book contains both some advice to singles and their "holy hunt" and some very practical advice for those who are already married. To some extent this book also covers the issue of raising children, but I have chosen not to focus too much on this since my kids are still teenagers and frankly we have not reached the finish line yet. The goal is that they will choose to love, follow and serve Jesus when they as adults leave our home, and that one day they too will build strong and healthy marriages and families.

This time I have chosen to write a book exclusively for believers and people who know and read their Bible. This book makes no claims of being complete, final or exhaustive in this area. On the contrary, this is my little contribution to all the other amazing literature that has been written on this topic. I thank God for all the good books about marriage and family that are out there. I hope that more people will grab a pen and write. The topic is so important and it affects us all, one way or another.

While I write I pray that this book will also save a few couples from divorce. My prayer is also that this book will find its way in to the hands of those who are desperately trying to repair their broken relationship. You need each other and above all, your children need you to stick together. Lord Jesus, do the miraculous!

Go ahead, read and contemplate!

Stockholm in November 2013

Johannes Amritzer
Leader, Mission SOS

CHAPTER 1

HOLY HUNT

He who finds a wife finds what is good and receives favor from the LORD.

Proverbs 18:22

This passage clearly speaks about the man who has found a wife. Before you can find something you have to search for it, right? Many believers think that if they only pray persistently, the beautiful princess will show up in their bachelor pad, waving and saying hello with a charming smile. Let me bring it to you as simple as I can, my friend: no matter how much you pray in your ugly, musty apartment, she will never find you. Look around! Garbage, filthy laundry and yellow, stained curtains in the kitchen. Who will be looking for you, as you sit there in the midst of empty milk cartons with no deodorant and dandruff on your shoulders? Yes, it all begins with prayer. Absolutely. But perhaps it's time to open a window, air out the odor of stinky feet, cut your hair and brush your teeth.

Seriously though. You are not going to marry an angel, but a wonderful person that is somewhere out there right now. This wonderful someone has a beating heart, dreams and hopes. This wonderful someone is eagerly waiting for you to show up.

Let me give you the Biblical order of "the holy hunt" from Jesus' famous Sermon on the Mount:

> *Ask and it will be given to you; seek and you will find; knock and the door will be opened to you.*
>
> **Matthew 7:7**

1. Start praying for a spouse every day!

2. Search; use binoculars to scan the hunting grounds, one by one!

3. Pound, or at least knock on her door and ask her out!

In several of the Old Testament texts it even says that the man "took a wife", which might be just a little too radical for the modern people of our time. But surely the expression to "take a wife" tells us that this whole starting a family thing was something that a man simply had to do when he had reached a certain age. Getting married was without doubt both a practical and hands-on act in the early days of humanity. Back then the parents and older relatives were involved in helping the children start a family when they had reached a certain age, and they seem to have loved matchmaking. As grateful as we are today that our modern time and culture allows us to choose life partners ourselves, we still ought to remember that the advice from parents and relatives is in no way irrelevant. Listen to the elderly and those with more experience, but choose to listen to your heart. After all, you are the one getting married - not your mom or dad. The Bible says:

> *Houses and wealth are inherited from parents, but a prudent wife is from the LORD.*
>
> **Proverbs 19:14**

This passage speaks about inheritance from the parents but it also clearly says that a wife is a gift directly from God. He wants to answer your intense prayers and give you a life partner as a gift but you have to do your part, you must search and hunt - but do it with the greatest respect. It may seem a bit contradictory, searching for a present, but think of it as though you are looking for an Easter egg or a buried treasure. I would like to give some pieces of advice to you who are single and ready to start the holy hunt. Think of the rest of this chapter as a "hunting license test". Soon you will have both a license and a gun in your hands - with the safety off!

ASK QUESTIONS

All dating and hunting for a life partner begins with many big questions. Ask a lot of questions before you get involved in a relationship. The answers to your honest and sincere thoughts are crucial as to whether or not the two of you can proceed toward engagement and wedding. The whole point of dating is for you to get answers to the most crucial questions as quickly as possible. The very idea of dating is to be curious and ferret out as much as possible about the person you are interested in.

I believe the three most important questions are:

1. Do we share the same calling and do our plans for the future match?

2. Do we have the same Christian theology, life style and somewhat similar opinions?

3. Do we have the same interests, humor and do we laugh together?

These three questions are about calling, faith and chemistry. Calling, faith and chemistry are crucial when it comes to building a strong marriage.

If these three areas do not match, the future relationship is often doomed even before it begins. Never compromise on this! These three keys must fit perfectly in the locks. The engine will break without oil. Sooner or later, you will be stranded by the side of the road if you use the wrong fuel. These three areas simply have to work!

As I'm sure you already understand, looking for a life partner that does not share your faith in God is out of the question. The Bible speaks very clearly about how impossible it is to unite a believer with a non-believer in a healthy marriage. Read this:

> *Do not be yoked together with unbelievers. For what do righteousness and wickedness have in common? Or what fellowship can light have with darkness?*
>
> **2 Corinthians 6:14**

Many have entered a relationship believing that that they would win their partner for God, but instead they signed up for a nightmare that ended in a catastrophe. Of course there are exceptions with happy endings, but do not take that chance. We are talking about the rest of your life. The choice of life partner is too big and much too crucial for you to gamble and just hope for the best. Do not marry a seeker, even if he or she says "perhaps one day I will find a faith in God". The seeker may find a different faith than the one you are hoping for. What if he chooses to go from being an Atheist to a Buddhist? Do not take such risks.

I think we need to take this one step further and go from the importance of sharing the faith, to really highlighting the importance of having the same calling and plans for the future. If you believe that God has called you to be a missionary to India but the person you start to date wants to start a business and open a new store in New York City, you will have trouble building a future together. Or you want to plant a church and she wants to run a business. Maybe you want to live in the slums of New Delhi while she wants to live in a penthouse on Manhattan. I'm not saying that one is more right or holy than the other. God calls some to plant churches and some, by the same God are called to run companies, but synchronizing those two rather diverse callings might not be easy.

The Bible tells us about Moses whose mission was to lead the Jews from slavery in Egypt to their own country where they would live in freedom. Moses almost died on his way to Egypt, because his wife Zipporah did not understand the meaning and importance of sharing her husband's calling (read Exodus 4:24-25). There is no real protection in a holy calling and spiritual ministry if it is not owned and carried by both spouses in a marriage.

The Bible also shares the success story in the New Testament about the Jewish couple Priscilla and Aquila who both preached, planted churches and trained disciples together. They stood united in the calling as missionaries. They served God together both as a couple and as a family (read Acts chapter 18). What an amazing and wonderful life they must have lived together in the center of the perfect will of God!

Having completely different Christian theology and doctrines can also become a huge problem in a relationship. One thinks it is really important to evangelize and do missions while the other thinks it is unnecessary to actively share your faith with others. A quiet, calm, and more meditative Christian might find it difficult to share life with a loud, charismatic, worshipping, dancing, and speaking-in-tongues Christian. If one is liberal when it comes to alcohol and the other is a teetotaler, then there will no doubt be constant conflicts at birthdays, holidays and when inviting friends over for dinner. Having the same, or almost the same theology and Christian life style is really important for a long and happy marriage.

Personal chemistry is also important - probably more important than you think. You are supposed to enjoy sitting at the same kitchen table every day for more than 50 years. It is crucial for a lifetime of happiness that you can understand one another, read one another and above all laugh hard together. Do not ignore the fact that you did not get a few spontaneous laughs on the first or second date. Do not pretend like you had a good time. The chemistry between the two of you is too important.

In the Old Testament there is a rather cute story of a couple living abroad due to a famine in their country. They are staying as King Abimelek's guests. Due to fear of being separated, Isaac and Rebekah lied, saying they were not married. Isaac was afraid that they would kill him and take Rebekah from him because she was so attractive, so he lies and tells everyone that Rebekah is his sister. Then the Bible says this:

> *When Isaac had been there a long time, Abimelek king of the Philistines looked down from a window and saw Isaac caressing his wife Rebekah.*
>
> **Genesis 26:8**

Isaac was caressing his wife Rebekah in public. An old Swedish translation from 1917 says that he was "playing lovingly" with her. I wonder what Isaac was doing with Rebekah? Did he playfully pinch her behind or...? It must have been something like that that the king saw when he looked out the window. It must have been something playful, something that only spouses do, right? Or else the king would not have exclaimed:

> *She is really your wife!*
>
> **Genesis 26:9**

Abimelek was sure of it. There was no doubt that Rebekah was Isaac's wife. The king had seen them making out and anything but them being married was out of the question. They were a couple - end of story.

My point is that Isaac and Rebekah must have had great chemistry! They were in love. They caressed one another; they made jokes and laughed the way only loved ones do. They had fun! They loved one another and they could not hide it! Husband and wife were exposed! They were hopelessly and wonderfully in love with each other.

DON'T RUSH IT

Getting married and starting a family is a big step. Who you will share your adult life with is a big deal. After salvation it is actually the most important and most holy decision you will ever make. You will exchange vows before God and people. You will even pledge eternal faithfulness. There may be many Mr. Right or Miss. Right before the day when you stand before God and the priest, but once you have said the words "I do" there will never be anyone else. It will be the two of you forever. Think about that. It does sound a bit fateful, does it not? Yes, my friend! It does! Jesus said:

> *Therefore, what God has joined together, let no one separate.*
>
> **Matthew 19:6**

You should not rush these things. Choose carefully, thoughtfully and with great respect. You only choose once. There is no rule stating that you need to get married within three months of starting a relationship or dating. But on the other hand, if there is a perfect match between the two of you, why wait. Do not try to please people in this area, neither in one direction nor the other. Follow the voice of God's Spirit in your heart! Every couple has their own path to walk before God that will lead up to vows being exchanged and the covenant sealed.

> *Do not be anxious about anything, but in every situation, by prayer and petition, with thanksgiving, present your requests to God. And the peace of God, which transcends all understanding, will guard your hearts and your minds in Christ Jesus.*
>
> **Philippians 4:6-7**

THE WISH LIST

Some Christian singles make a prayer list or wish list of how their knight in shining armor or princess girl will look like and then they wait for that perfect person to show up. There is just one catch: if that knight in shining armor or princess girl also has a written list of qualifications, you will not stand a chance, will you? You have to be realistic and you must dare to review yourself critically. Look deep into the mirror, my friend. If you are a number 5 on the "good-looking-scale", do not aim for Miss 9 or 10. You too have flaws, you are not 100% satisfied with everything, so do not require too much of your partner - or else you will never get married. Choose the kind one over the good-looking. Choose the one that makes you laugh over the one with all the money. Choose the grateful one over the spoiled one. Choose the one with no prestige over the proud one. Choose character over beauty. Remember that maybe there will be no game of picking and choosing. Who are you to have such high demands? Well, you might say, "Only the best is good enough for me." Question is, are you the best of the best for someone else? Take it down a notch. Be humble. You will indeed be happily married if you just dare to think right.

WAITING FOR A SIGN?

Some people are waiting for that very special divine sign. Rainbows will cross and stars fall. Meteoroids will light up the evening sky and he or she will in that very moment say the exact words of your choice. Sure, God can give you a sign! Signs are Biblical, even though God first and foremost speaks to us directly through his Holy Spirit on the inside and not through signs. The Bible tells us the story of how Abraham's servant Eliezer asks for a sign when he was looking for a wife for his master's son Isaac (read Gen 24:12-14). In this particular story Eliezer was looking for character over beauty and God gave Isaac both in Rebekah. Rebekah was a girl with a servant's attitude and she was also ready to work hard if needed. She was beautiful but above all had character.

Charm is deceptive, and beauty is fleeting; but a woman who fears the LORD is to be praised.

Proverbs 31:30

Some are stuck with all four tires deep in the mud. They are so focused on waiting for the "sign" that they miss the gift that God has given and placed right in front of them. Someone said: "Everything matches, but it doesn't feel right". If everything matches maybe you should not be so emotional. Instead believe that love will grow once you go all in. If the calling, faith and personal chemistry match, but that special sign you asked for has still not been seen in the sky, do not be over spiritual and foolish but start a relationship anyway. Feelings can be deceiving. Do not follow the roller coaster of the soul - follow the voice of your heart, God's Spirit in your spirit.

UNCLEAN MOTIVES

Be careful and do understand that not every man or woman out there is completely honest. There are people who have unclean motives and want to get married for the wrong reasons. Some people think of marriage as a way to that permanent residency they have been longing for. Someone else pretends to be the person you desire, but is really someone else. Do not allow yourself to be manipulated or seduced. Know your value and take the necessary dating time very seriously. You need to have time to ask all of your questions and to really get to know the person behind the façade, however charming the person may seem on the first date. Do not hold hands, hug or kiss until you know that this really is a relationship that you want and dare to go on with. Do not sell out too cheap or too quickly. Do not end up in bed with some charming princess just because you could not resist. Embrace and value your purity.

I'm sad to say that over the years as a pastor I have had to pick up the pieces of broken hearts after big disappointments so many times. Maria and I have often desperately tried to patch the deceived and far too credulous person back together. Because of this, I have to be very clear on this matter.

She got pregnant and he left both her and the child alone without even trying to help out financially. It all started with big promises about how they would live for God together and ended up with her sitting alone and abandoned in a small apartment in the hood. He was too new in the Christian faith. Or, in a different scenario, her loyalty to the Swedish culture and the subtle, subconscious prejudice racist thoughts were too strong and deeply rooted and his loyalty toward his family in his home country turned out to be much stronger than she thought. Yes, life can be real tough, cold and harsh. Now she has lost her virginity, and all the money that she received from her mom and dad for her new home is gone.

"She said she had tested negative for HIV but that wasn't true. Why did I have unprotected sex with her? How could I have been so naive?"

"I never should have trusted that girl. She was so charming and said all the right things. Why didn't I listen to my big sister? She told me... I should have known better. Daddy warned me. How could I have been so stupid?"

The list goes on. Do not destroy your life. Not everyone is honest. That is the blunt reality.

WARNING SIGNS

There are warning signs that you should to take seriously. Let me give you a few examples:

1. When he or she says: "I don't want us to hang out with your family or your best friends". Remember that your family and your best friends are your safety net and your greatest protection in life. A predator always tries to isolate his prey from the flock before it scratches, strikes and kills.

2. When he or she says: "This is our secret. Promise me you won't tell anyone". No, my friend. If he has abused you, you have to tell

your dad or older brother! In every culture dad and big brother are actually the lady's natural protection. There are no secrets too delicate for you to share with your closest ones, if you feel that you should.

3. When you hear strange explanations and evasions, when you keep getting mixed signals and he or she constantly tells small white lies. Remember that if he or she is lying to others, chances are he or she is also lying to you.

4. When he or she is upset just because you want to see a receipt or want evidence and the person says: "You don't trust me! You are just jealous and antsy". Remember that trust is built over time and grows stronger every time you are open and honest toward one another. A relationship that begins with arguments and in distrust is bound to fail.

If you feel like there is a heavy stone in your belly and an uneasiness that will not let go, just end the relationship right away. End it before that other person has his claws so deep in your soul that you cannot get out. You will not become abandoned and alone just because you say no to one or two proposers. Believe that God has the best person in store for you!

Make sure you do not let racism take root so that you judge all Asian people because you were let down by a Thai girl. Dishonest people come in all colors and they exist in every culture. Likewise, there are honest and truthful people in all countries and the love of your life may be found where you least expect it. Do not allow disappointment and bitterness to close any doors for you, but stay open even after you hit a landmine. We do not let fear of snakes hinder us from trekking outdoors, and we do not stop driving our car because a moron who was driving under the influence killed someone. We continue to believe the best. We choose to believe that the "great love" is out there for you, my friend. Have you failed or been let down? Wipe your tears now. There is happiness for you as well.

CAN SHE HUNT?

I know that by now many of my readers have already asked this question. I'm sure you are wondering if it is only the man who is supposed to take the initiative. Can girls hunt or is that task for him alone? I believe that the most natural thing is for the man to be the "hunter", and not the woman. I believe that certain roles are planted deep within us, living within our DNA and the human nature that God has given us. Male and female is not solely a matter of how children are raised - it is created by God and gets activated in the early teens. He should initiate the first step. Many guys will have to get rid of their cowardice and start making some moves. Perhaps there is a happily married lady reading this, that felt she could not wait any longer, and decided to take matters in her own hands. There are many such examples. Do not think too much about that - just be happy! But I still think it's a shame that women need to run out and hunt for guys. Conquering comes naturally to the man and the desire to be taken by storm comes naturally to the woman. Someone said that if she is not going to hunt, then at least she could send out clear signals. You are right! Girls! If you are interested, make sure you show it loud and clear and remember that most guys are rather slow in this area. Send very clear signals, but let him believe that he took the initiative so that he will feel like a real man.

Yes, this is how the game and dynamics between man and woman has worked for thousands of years. Therefore I would like to close this chapter by encouraging all guys to dare to be men and to actually take the initiative and start asking girls out. Put this book down for a few moments and give her a call right away! Do not wait! How could a good movie followed by a cup of coffee ever be a bad idea? It is not the end of the world if it ends with just being a nice evening out with very cute company. The answers to some simple questions will decide if and how you will proceed from there. Now you know what to look for, right? But first you are actually just supposed to laugh together and open-mindedly build friendship. It is as simple as that. The trick and key to your success with the holy hunt is your sincerity, your lack of prestige and if you dare to be yourself. Be relaxed and respectful when you date. Have fun without breaking anyone's heart. Enjoy without going too far, creating false expectations or just flirting. Good luck!

Joseph: "Pregnant through the Holy Spirit?! Yeah, sure baby..."

CHAPTER 2

THE FAMILY IS GOD'S PLAN

When God staged His salvation plan He did it, as we all know, through a virgin birth. A virgin birth was something that had never happened before in the history of humanity. The news about Mary's supernatural pregnancy must have come as a complete shock to everyone involved in this family drama (read Matthew 1:18-25 or Luke 1:26-38).

The young and newly engaged Mary is suddenly pregnant and she blames the Holy Spirit. She talks about an angelic visitation and it sounds really confusing and crazy. Who will believe her?

Joseph, a man of honor, has already come up with a plan to divorce her in secret. But then he has this vivid and spiritual dream. In the dream he too is visited by an angel that brings him the same message as his girl Mary has received. The child is from the Holy Spirit and they have received a holy task and responsibility. The Messiah will be born,

His name will be Jesus and He will save His people from their sins. They are a chosen family and the child growing inside Mary is the Savior of the world!

Yes, that is how God let His Son become a human being. God needed two secure parents and a stable marriage to stage His salvation plan. I often say that the family is God's ingenious plan to save the world. Without a strong family it would not have been possible for God to send His Son to us to save us.

We find the key building blocks for a strong and sound family in the Scripture passages in Matthew and Luke (mentioned above). To build a strong family you need:

1. Faith in God

2. Trust and confidence

3. Mutual protection

Faith, trust and protection are the three most important building blocks and together they create the perfect environment and atmosphere for children to be raised.

Mary and Joseph had a strong faith in God. They believed that angels could come with messages and they believed in the work and influence of the Holy Spirit. Mary and Joseph believed in miracles! I'm sure a strong faith in God was nurtured in their home as they read the Holy Scriptures out loud and prayed and worshipped God together as a family.

God was a natural part of their family life. The children lived with the safety, warmth, gratitude and humility that only a faith in God can create. Mary and Joseph were chosen by God for this very reason - their strong faith in God.

Mary and Joseph also showed a great trust in one another. Just the fact that Joseph chose to believe Mary's story of how she had become pregnant through the Holy Spirit is really exceptionally impressive. With or without Joseph's angelic visitation, his trust in Mary is incredible. Talk about trust! There seems to be no trace of suspicion and jealousy, but on the contrary a deep gratitude that they were specially chosen by God. They chose to believe in each other. They chose to trust one another.

> *It [love] always protects, always trusts, always hopes, always perseveres.*
>
> **1 Corinthians 13:7**

Mary and Joseph also protected each other. They had their family secrets. Surely only Mary and Joseph knew that Jesus was not really their own son but the Son of God. I do not think they told their parents, relatives or close friends. They did not want Nasareth to find out the secret of whose son Jesus really was. They knew that not everyone would understand if they were told the truth, maybe they would not even want to understand. Sometimes the truth is simply too difficult and complex for the general public's insensitivity and the cold, harsh society. Mary needed Joseph's strong integrity and more so, his protection and loyalty. No one could know. Joseph would not tolerate people's judgmental words about his Mary. No one was allowed to discredit his wife or gossip about her having had some other man before him. No. The child was his, end of story. Jesus needed a safe mom and dad who did not chatter with everyone.

In a cold and often cynical society both spouses need protection - not to mention the children. In a time when people lack the fear of God and when journalists, vultures and hyenas happily tear a family to pieces there is a very real need of protection. Do you want to build a strong marriage and a stable family? Make sure you lay the right foundation from the start! The three most important building blocks are faith in God, trust and protection.

In the Old Testament of the Bible we find the story of Moses becoming the mighty deliberator of the Jewish people. God told Moses to lead His people from slavery to freedom. At the time of Moses' birth, King Pharaoh of Egypt wanted to kill all little boys and throw them to the crocodiles in the Nile River. But Moses' parents hid and protected their boy. When Jesus was born King Herod tried to kill all boys under the age of two, but Jesus' parents went on a two-year exile to Egypt, to save their son's life. Parents protect their children if the marriage and the family are built properly from the beginning.

The family is the "little church" and the church/congregation is the big family. The church reflects the family and the family reflects Jesus' (the groom's) relationship with us, His bride.

It is all linked together. The families are the building blocks of society! Without stable families there is no society. We need to take a stand for families! The family is under attack in today's western society. The family is holy. The family is strong when it sticks together. The family is the foundation for all fellowship and cohesion. When spouses pray together and trust and protect one another, the little family is a power broker just as the big family - the church.

> *Unless the LORD builds the house, the builders labor in vain. Unless the LORD watches over the city, the guards stand on watch in vain. In vain you raise early and stay up late, toiling for food to eat - for he grants sleep to those he loves. Children are a heritage from the LORD, offspring a reward from him.*
>
> **Psalm 127:1-3**

Let God join in building your house. Let God be a part of building your family. God wants to help and protect. Do not work in vain 24/7. Make Him your friend and He will bless you, even when you are sleeping. God promises a great reward to those spouses who build a strong family. Your children grow up and could impact the entire nation, given the right prerequisites. Never speak negatively about your partner. Never correct your partner or your children in front of others. Protect the honor of your partner and your children. Remember that the family is God's plan to save the world!

$6 \div 2(1+2) = ?$
$(3y^2+1)(3y^2-1)^0$
$1+1=$
$\frac{\sqrt{81}}{3} =$
$\sqrt{64}$
π
10^5
$\frac{x}{7}+3=?$
$E=MC^2$
GAS

CHAPTER 3

AMRITZER'S MARRIAGE FORMULA

May God himself, the God of peace, sanctify you through and through. May your whole spirit, soul and body be kept blameless at the coming of our Lord Jesus Christ.

1 Thessalonians 5:23

God created us as spirit, soul and body. Human beings are spirit, soul and body. Of course man and woman are independent individuals, but together they make a whole once they have given their vows before God. Together they reflect the character of God. Both male and female is found in our Creator, even though the Bible refers to Him as Father. Therefore marriage reflects God better than a single does. It actual says:

So God created mankind in his own image, in the image of God he created them; male and female he created them.

Genesis 1:27

When man and woman are united they begin to create and reproduce themselves just like God does. A single cannot, as we all know, reproduce. Man and woman create by conceiving and giving birth to babies. This is what the story of the creation tells us:

> *God blessed them and said to them, "Be fruitful and increase in number; fill the earth and subdue it".*
>
> **Genesis 1:28**

We will get back to talking about children in a later section of this book. Now I would like to highlight the unity and fellowship between a man and a woman. The unique and wonderful thing about marriage is found in the union of man and woman. Male and female in harmony and in an inseparable covenant contain both creative power and likeness with God. Two spirits, two souls, and two bodies are to be united and begin to have fellowship. Since they continue to be two individuals even after the marriage ceremony, they can never stop nurturing fellowship in each of these three areas. To remain strong and faithful in their marriage the spouses continuously need to unite in spirit, soul and body. God has created us in this shrewd and wonderful way and our fellowship needs to be cultivated in this divine order. If there is no spiritual fellowship, then the mental (soul) fellowship will suffer and the physical fellowship will be shallow and self-indulgent.

S
M
P
S
M
P
S
M
P
S
M
P

THE MARRIAGE FORMULA

Many couples start off totally wrong. They turn God's orders upside down and start with body, then soul, and spiritually – well maybe... This messes things up and will make it difficult to regain balance later in life, even after honest attempts. Many have failed but still managed to get back on track. The gospel is all about forgiveness and a second change, even many chances to new beginnings. Perhaps you as a reader have started in the wrong end. Don't be discouraged. You can start over, my friend. Fellowship between a man and a woman that are about to enter marriage should be cultivated in the right order; that is spirit, soul and then body, not the other way around. Sex is a confirmation and a sign that a covenant has been entered. The physical unity is a covenant-act, a proclamation, and a feast on the wedding night after vows before God and witnesses.

After many years as a pastor, many pre-wedding counseling sessions, and weddings and only God knows how many hours of marriage counseling, I have come up with a simple marriage formula. To some extent it is a tongue-in-cheek formula that should be received with a grain of salt and a smile. Anyway, here it is: Amritzer's marriage formula:

2 X (S+M+P) / WEEK

EXPLANATION:

2 = 2 x 60 minutes of fellowship

s = spiritual fellowship

m = mental (soul) fellowship

p = physical (body) fellowship

MY EXPERIENCE FROM MARRIAGE COUNSELING:

Level 1: 1 x (s+m+p) / week = a surviving marriage at a minimum level (starvation)

Level 2: 2 x (s+m+p) / week = a good marriage in harmony

Level 3: 3 x (s+m+p) / week = a very healthy marriage

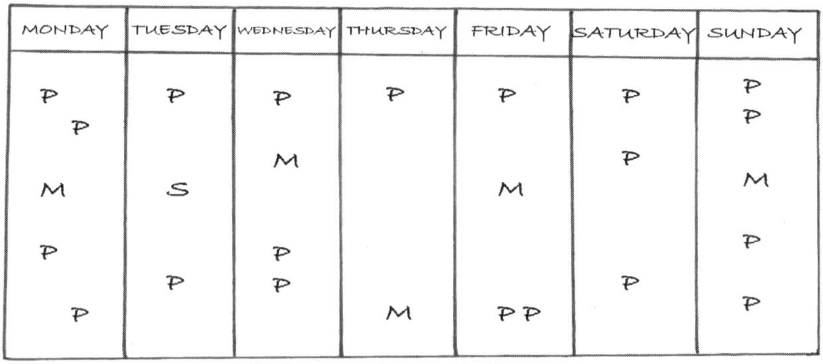

1.) The newly weds´first calendar

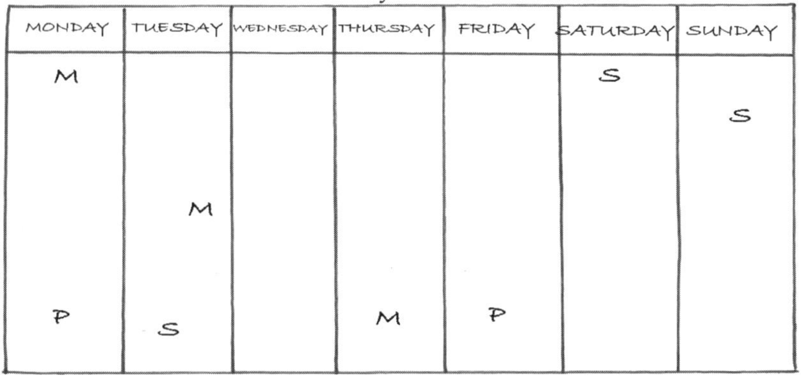

2.) Married for 5 years

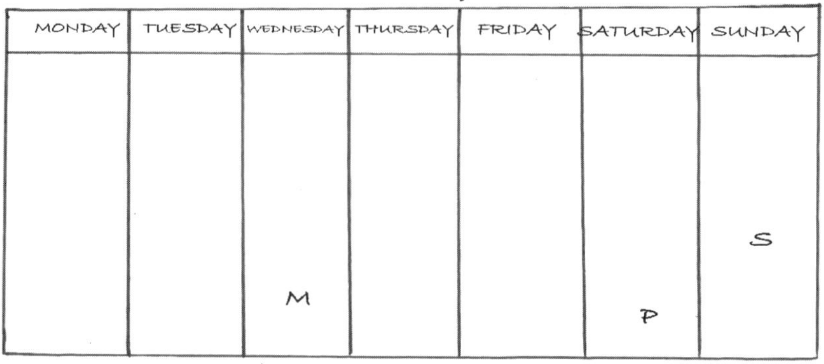

3.) Married for 10 years

CHECK THE TEMPERATURE OF YOUR MARRIAGE

Many of the couples that I have wed have, in the beginning of their marriage, actually written a small s, m or p in their calendars every time they have had one of the three types of fellowship. But I recommend that you do it again after a few years. Yes, keep doing it now and then just to really check how your marriage is doing. Do it this coming month to check the temperature of your marriage. If you suspect that you are weak in one area, find out which and make sure you strengthen your marriage in that area. A marriage survey every now and then is absolutely necessary. Maybe all you need to do is change the oil and filter and recharge your batteries for the engine to run smoothly again. Think of it as a three thousand mile service on your car and then apply this analogy to your marriage. A service and a thorough check once a year is a must in order to maintain a strong marriage. This book is written to prevent the crisis. I am writing because I believe it is possible to have a successful marriage, but not without hard work from both of you. Visit your repair shop and a mechanic if you have to. But start by checking the oil and coolant levels yourselves first - if you also need to top up your washer fluid you can do that without counseling.

Everything below level one is usually a marriage in crisis and in desperate need of counseling and immediate help.

Some people limp in one or two areas but they still need help to find their way back to harmony and balance in their relationship. Perfect harmony is reached when both spouses cultivate fellowship and approximately the same amount of time is spent on each slice in the illustration below. Starvation in one area is devastating for the other two and it affects and interrupts more than you think. Since we as human beings are spirit, soul and body in one harmonious union, then each part will affect the others. Balance and harmony must be protected, maintained and desired. If you after your marriage survey realize you are below level one, do not wait: find counseling and help.

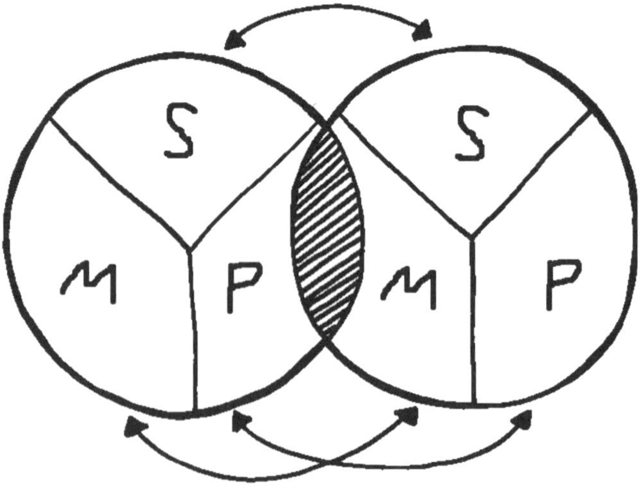

WHAT DOES YOUR LIST LOOK LIKE?

Begin to define what spiritual, mental (soul), and physical (body) fellowship means to you both individually. A man's list can be very different from a woman's. Make your own list, both of you. As step two, sit down together and look at your lists. Compare the two and try to agree on what you can and want to do together in order to cultivate a strong fellowship in every area.

The man's list can look like this:

SPIRITUAL FELLOWSHIP:

Pray and read the Bible together every Saturday morning.

Go to church together every Sunday.

Go on a mission trip together once a year.

MENTAL (SOUL) FELLOWSHIP:

Have a date night once a week.

Buy a motorcycle and go for rides together.

Get a gym membership and work out together twice a week.

PHYSICAL (BODY) FELLOWSHIP:

Well… Have sex every day?! Yes! Yay!

The woman's list can look like this:

SPIRITUAL FELLOWSHIP:

Read a spiritual book together and talk about what we have read.

Sit down on the couch and worship Jesus together as a family.

Join a small group together.

MENTAL (SOUL) FELLOWSHIP:

Take a nutrition class together.

Play the board game Risk with the whole family.

Go shopping at the mall together.

PHYSICAL (BODY) FELLOWSHIP:

Bubble bath together in the Jacuzzi with scented candles.

Make love outdoors in a meadow after a bike ride in the summer.

Lie on the pier in the sunset while kissing and caressing each other.

The lists can vary quite a bit depending on interests, background and preferences. Your list will most likely be different from your partner's, mainly because you are man and woman. The lists will also change as your life together goes through different seasons such as the time before kids, the toddler years, the teenage years, when you are middle aged and when you are senior citizens.

After completing your lists the search for mutual activities that are stimulating and fun for both of you begins. An activity where one of you suffer through will not build your relationship in the long haul, even though sacrificing a bit for the other can be beneficial every now and then. The key is to talk. Communication is crucial. Talk about what you both prefer and think you would like to try. Dare to be curious, inventive and always open to trying new things together. Just learning to talk about everything can be such a revolution in a relationship. Talk about spiritual and mental (soul) fellowship, and dare to talk about sex. Talk to each other!

Some will say that they have tried to make 2 x (s+m+p) per week work, but that a whole hour per occasion is impossible. Remember then that this is a guide toward something better, and hopefully you will find your own unique marriage formula in time. Your formula might look different from ours. The most important thing is to reach balance and harmony between the spirit, soul, and body and the fellowship that needs to be cultivated between the two of you.Good luck!

ACTION POINTS

Sit down and make a list of what you think is good spiritual, mental (soul), and physical (body) fellowship.

HIS LIST

SPIRITUAL FELLOWSHIP

MENTAL (SOUL) FELLOWSHIP

PHYSICAL (BODY) FELLOWSHIP

HER LIST

SPIRITUAL FELLOWSHIP

MENTAL (SOUL) FELLOWSHIP

PHYSICAL (BODY) FELLOWSHIP

1
25
10
LOVE
GAS

CHAPTER 4
THE LOVE ACCOUNT

My beloved is mine and I am his…

Song of Solomon 2:16 A

Do you want to build a lifelong and happy marriage? Do you want the two of you to be best friends in 20 years? It is possible! It really is! It has worked for us. Do not take for granted that your love and happiness will continue over the years, but instead realize that it requires regular investments over and over again.

You need to start saving. To save and store up is the secret to happiness when your marriage reaches its second half. The Bible says:

Dishonest money dwindles away, but whoever gathers money little by little makes it grow.

Proverbs 13:11

Saving is holy and not just “a little” blessed. This is so important to God that it actually says that He commands blessings over our storehouses.

> *The Lord will command the blessing on you in your storehouses and in all to which you set your hand, and He will bless you in the land which the Lord your God is giving you.*
>
> **Deuteronomy 28:8 NKJV**

When we choose to follow God’s principles in the Bible, His favor and bonus is poured out as a wet kiss from heaven, a modern way to say blessed by God. But saving is so holy in the eyes of God that it is written that He will ”command the blessing” on your storehouses and savings for your future! ”Commanded blessings” are actually only mentioned three times in the Bible. Commanded blessings are related to:

1. Rest (Lev 25)
2. Fellowship (Ps 133)
3. Saving (Deut 28)

God Himself promises to command blessing on those who dare to follow these three principles. Can you see God sitting on His throne commanding the angels to help those who practice rest, fellowship and saving?

So what in the world does this have to do with marriage? Well, marriage contains these three blessed components. Marriage and family is supposed to be the castle in which you rest and regain your strength, and where you are protected by a strong, intimate fellowship. Marriage and family is also the perfect storehouse for you when you grow old. Your spouse and especially your children will appreciate that you save money. But let me tell you about a different kind of saving. If you dare to practice what I will now try to explain you will live a life constantly followed by everything that is good. I have chosen to call this marriage recipe for The Love Account.

THERE IS AN ACCOUNT IN YOUR NAME IN YOUR SPOUSE'S HEART

In my dear Maria's heart there is an account entitled "Johannes' love account" and in my heart there is a pink safety deposit box named "Maria's treasure trove". Continue reading and the different names will make sense. Let me briefly explain to you how deposits and withdrawals, interests and fees work in the love bank that is called marriage.

Every time I show my love verbally, practically or by sacrificing a little bit of my comfort for my spouse, I make a deposit in my love account in my darling's heart. Both small and large deposits are constantly made in every day life. After many years of consistent deposits, a huge love fund accumulates. The story of Joseph in Egypt (Gen 37-50) is an amazing example of divinely inspired saving that eventually rescued both the nation and the neighboring countries from starvation death. We save during the good years in order to survive the bad years of starvation, just like the story of Joseph teaches us. A long life has both years of rich and plentiful harvest, but also years of drought and flooding. The Bible teaches us in a hands-on way how we are to survive the storms and barren seasons of life. Your marriage will survive the tough years if you invest a lot while you can. Invest while the sun is still shining on you as you walk hand in hand on the beach, young and strong. Invest during the good years!

DIFFERENT LOVE LANGUAGES

As individuals we all speak different love languages. This means that we give and respond differently when it comes to showing love, tenderness and appreciation. I need verbal encouragement, such as "Wow, you look so good! Well-built and tanned!" Two sentences like that can make my whole day! I am that silly. Hearing something like that can make me run on a euphoric energy boost for days. I appreciate a carefully penned letter or a love declaration on the back of a beautiful card. Then I bring the card with me for months wherever I go. It sits in my Bible or in the inner pocket of my leather jacket and I read it over and over again. Often I fall asleep in a hotel bed with the card on my chest only to wake up with the card all crinkled at the foot of the bed. I smooth it out, read it again, wipe a few tears and then carefully put it back in my Bible. A card like that from my Maria or perhaps my daughter is very holy to me. I also appreciate a gift. Oh my, how silly I can get over a nice gift. I keep the watch in the box it came in every time I'm not using it. After five years it can still look brand new. Well, that's how I am. Perhaps it is because gifts and appreciative words were few in my life when I was growing up but I do not know for sure and I am no expert on the deepest needs of the human soul. But today I do know a little bit about how I function as a human being and what makes me really happy and feel good.

My precious Maria speaks a different love language and needs to feel that I am there for her and that I give her and the children some "holy" time; private quality time with just the family. She tells me that the fence needs to be repaired and painted and I make it happen. I make arrangements with a painter and I go buy lumber. She is so happy! She happens to mention that we are out of firewood or that she is longing for a vacation under the Turkish sun and I purchase both wood and tickets. She is so happy and loving! She shines and laughs for weeks when I manage to speak her love language! She is so down to earth, simple and practical. I love her for that. Without her practical and hands-on love our children's homework would not get done, and our son Adam would not have that warm winter coat. She has created that cozy home that I never knew or understood that we needed, until she gave us one. She proved that I was wrong and that I really did not know it all. Maria has taught me that no one will build a home on the road. I am an adventurer and globetrotter to the core, but found peace when Maria built us a home. Thank you Maria! Where would I (we) be without you?

I'm not really talking about flowers and chocolate here. I hope you understand that in a stable marriage nothing can be bought so easily, in a charming and flirty "Don Juan" way. I started off that way but quickly realized that it did not work. Flowers, perfume, and jewelry are just bonuses in your lives but no real investments in your marriage. Be charming, but let it be the "little extra" and the final spice in the stew before you place the food on the table. No one can live on spices alone, you can actually live without them, although it will get boring in the long run. The Bible says so wisely about sowing and reaping:

> *"Do not be deceived, God is not mocked; for whatever a man sows, that he will also reap."*
>
> **Galatians 6:7**

WITHDRAWALS FROM THE LOVE BANK

Let your secret treasure in the heart of your loved one grow and accumulate great wealth. You will need that saving. Continue to sow and you will reap. You might need your savings a lot faster than you think. Your savings in the love account can decrease so quickly and you will be poor again. What are you talking about, Johannes? You see, life doesn't always run on a golden highway and according to our time table.

Three years ago I had an accident with my motorcycle and distorted my right knee. Both medial and lateral ligaments were ripped off, the meniscus was torn apart and bone splinters came off. I waited for my first surgery for 19 days. I screamed in pain every time someone just touched my leg. I was on morphine for two months and it was all a rather blue mist. I was angry, moody and stupid. After my second knee surgery and long rehab I came back to my normal self. Both my family and I lived in some sort of martial law for a little over six months. It was no fun at all, even though my friends were extra kind to me and came over to play chess and have coffee with me. My family suffered. Maria and the kids were tip-toeing around me. The husband and father was a wounded lion that growled a lot and just could not live with himself. But we survived! We even grew stronger as a family. Personally I think the reason why we survived is because we had already been saving and investing in one another's love accounts for many years. There were enough funds to get through six months of sickness. My savings in Maria's and the children's hearts decreased, but it was never below minimum. It was truly months of big withdrawals and rather expensive fees. But I had been saving. What a family I have! Thank you for bearing with me, wonderful Amritzer family, even through the dark days!

All of a sudden your mom or dad gets really sick and they need you more during the last couple of months of their lives. You enter a time of life when you will have to forsake your spouse somewhat. Your children may not get the same attention and as much quality time as they are used to during these different seasons of hospital visits, goodbyes, comforting and preparations for a funeral. Your sister or brother suffers through a heart breaking divorce and you want to be there for them. Many unexpected things will happen in life. Those who once were strong can no longer make it on their own. All of a sudden your wife needs back surgery due to a herniated disc. Your teenager goes through a crisis that requires all of your attention. Your health fails and you need six months to recover. You are barren and after lots of struggle and many salty tears you decide to adopt. Suddenly things just do not work in your bedroom; your sex life is shipwrecked and you need to seek help. I could make the list so much longer.

SAVE, SAVE, SAVE!

Perhaps you who read this are mumbling to yourself: "I need to start saving". Yes! You are right! You need to start saving, because the evil days will come. The Bible is clear on this. I want to speak faith but I also want to help you build so firmly that you will survive the days when you simply do not have the energy to speak faith. I want to help you in the most honest way I can. I choose to be very practical, vulnerable and open in this book, so that we all can win. You and I will celebrate a gold anniversary, right?!

The Bible says:

> *Therefore take up the whole armor of God, that you may be able to withstand* ***in the evil day****, and having done all, to stand.*
>
> **Ephesians 6:13 (emphasis by author)**

Life is a battle. You are born a victor! You are destined to win the war! Prepare by building muscles and your future. Therefore invest and save now!

How do you save? You want to build a strong marriage and a solid family, right? I'm sure you are saying: "Tell me more! Give me more examples!" Here are a few extra examples from our every day life:

I come home late from the airport and get into bed beside my Maria. It is 2 AM. She is getting up at 5:30 AM to be a mom and a nurse. Her day will begin in just a few hours. I have been working abroad for several weeks and I have been longing for home. I have a day off tomorrow but she does not. Now I want to have sex and I am kind of into it already. She is tired, I mean really tired! I guess I realize that, and say that we can wait until tomorrow night instead. But my darling says: "No, come here Hannes". And she gives me the love that I need and have been longing for. She just deposited a big pile of selfless love in her account in my heart. While we fall asleep spooning I'm thinking, "Maria, you are the best girl in the world", before I drop off to sleep.

> *"Let your fountain be blessed, and rejoice with the wife of your youth"*
>
> **Proverbs 5:18**

Another time she dressed up in a skirt and high heels on a regular day. I ask her if I have missed anything. Are we expecting someone? Are we going out? She answers: "No, just because I love you!" This warms the most inner rooms of my heart. Maria masters the art of investing and saving. I will let her continue to teach us through the life that she lives every day. She does the laundry, irons the clothes, mows the lawn and drives our children to where they need to be. She cooks and lights candles. She loves us and she lives for us. She does not think I always see this, but I do. I see more than you know, honey! With God you have a greater treasure than everybody I know. In my heart you are a billionaire!

Maria has never demanded 50/50 equality in our relationship, and she has never counted how many times more than me she has emptied the dishwasher or cooked. I am very impressed by her spiritual maturity and strength. Maria invests. My darling makes deposits all the time. And because of that Maria does not have a small account in my heart, but a big pink safety deposit box - actually a a treasure chest full of pure gold.

ACTION POINT

Sit down and make a list of how you can make deposits in your spouse's love account. Be creative and enjoy it!

MONTHLY BUDGET		
INCOME	ASSUMED	ACTUAL
WORK	$	$
OTHER	$	$
EXPENSES	ASSUMED	ACTUAL
LIVING	$	$
CAR	$	$
FOOD	$	$
CLOTHES	$	$
FUN	$	$
OTHER	$	$
TOTAL	$	$

LOVE ACCOUNT		
	HIM	HER
DEPOSIT	CLEAN THE GUTTERS GO TO THE MOVIES GIFTS TIME	COOK SEXY LINGERIE COMPLIMENTS HOBBIES
	HIM	HER
WITHDRAWAL	BAD DAY OVERTIME	NAGGING
TOTAL	♡ ♡ ♡	♡ ♡ ♡ ♡ ♡

HIS ACCOUNT

HER ACCOUNT

HOO!
GAS

CHAPTER 5
HIM AND HER

So God created man in his own image; in the image of God he created him; male and female He created them.

Genesis 1:27

Male and female are very obvious and natural human concepts. Since there has been a rather fierce debate about male and female over the last several decades, we barely dare to speak about it anymore. Both male and female originated from the Creator, and the gender roles have clear guidelines and boundaries in the Bible. We need to study them extra thoroughly now since today's society does everything it can to erase the concepts. In other words, it is time to dig up an old obvious Biblical teaching about man and woman and their roles and responsibilities in marriage and family life. Dad needs to be dad and mom needs to be mom. Children need both a mother and a father.

HIM

Let us begin our teaching with how true manhood is defined in the Bible. Apostle Paul writes to men at the end of First Corinthians:

> *Watch, stand fast in the faith, be brave, be strong. Let all that you do be done with love.*
>
> **1 Corinthians 16:13-14**

According to Apostle Paul and the verses above, a Biblical man should be:

1. Watchful and protective

2. Firm in the faith

3. Brave and strong

4. Loving

A man should be on his guard; it has always been his task and role to watch over and protect his family. That is how my Austrian dad raised my brother and I. We had four younger sisters and lots of younger cousins. When we were just 11-12 years old dad told us: "When I am not around, it is your responsibility to protect your younger siblings and cousins." Dad's words were etched into my backbone. Several times as a teenager I fought to protect my flirty cousin Alexandra, who was my age. Keeping track of her was not an easy job,

I tell you! A real man is also expected to be firm in his convictions and opinions and not change with every new idea. To dodge questions and trim the sails to the wind is not the slight bit manly. If you dare to stand for what you have said and done, even when it costs you something, then you are a man. To admit being wrong, to ask for forgiveness, and without any prestige change your opinion after proven wrong is also manly. To be firm in your faith in God and stick to theology, doctrines and Biblical ethics and morals in a godless society also requires a big portion of manhood. "We stand where we stand", that's what my father used to say. "They know our position", he used to say and then we knew there was nothing anyone could do to change it. Being brave and strong is manly. We do not run and hide, we take a confrontation if we have to and we fight with our fists if needed. I can hear the voice of my South European dad in my head as I write this, and I am grateful for everything he taught me.

At the age of 19, an African friend and I went behind a school to pee. When we came around the corner of the school building, we saw something strange in the tall grass. Eight guys were ripping the underwear off a 14-year-old girl, and one of the guys already had her jeans in his hands. Five of the guys held her to the ground, and the other three were standing next to them. The girl was crying, biting at everything, desperately trying to get loose. They were eight. We were two. We never hesitated, not for a second. My dad's words were etched in my backbone. The idea that there might be knives or guns never crossed out minds.

We attacked simultaneously and well coordinated, like two panthers. We fought and screamed until we had rescued the girl. I am still very proud that we were able to save her. I am proud of every punch I threw that day and I am proud of every bruise I got. When the guys ran away, I looked the other way as I gave the girl her underwear and jeans back. We asked if she wanted us to walk her home. She said no, so we followed her at a distance until we saw her enter the building where she lived. We were young men. We were proud of what we had done - as we should have been. We did what was right and we received lots of compliments from both friends and relatives. I still think this type of moral courage is a must, and I teach my son Adam to do the same should he ever find himself in that kind of situation.

HE LOVES

Another thing that is very manly is to love, and to show love. Sacrificial love is manly in every sense of the word. That is the man's first and foremost responsibility in a marriage. Apostle Paul says:

> *Husbands, love your wives, just as Christ also loved the church and gave Himself for her…*
>
> **Ephesians 5:25**

Being macho and tough towards one's wife or children is not manly at all - it only destroys and breaks down the family.

Love builds. Sacrificial love is maximized manhood in its purest form.

> *Husbands, love your wives and do not be bitter toward them.*
>
> **Colossians 3:19**

A man who really loves his family will watch over it. He will be protective, firm, brave and strong. Love is the foundation of everything that is manly. Taking care of one's own and creating an Eden is every man's primary responsibility. When Apostle Paul speaks about how they behaved as leaders in the church he writes:

> *For you know how, like a father with his children, we exhorted each one of you and encouraged you and charged you…*
>
> **1 Thessalonians 2:11-12 (ESV)**

HE EXHORTS AND ENCOURAGES

In this scripture we find two other attributes that are typical for a man. The scripture describes the role and task that a dad has toward his children, namely to:

1. Exhort
2. Encourage

Exhort means to warn, strengthen, instill and correct - all at the same time. A dad exhorts and teaches the children how life should and should not be lived. My dad exhorted me and told me things I still remember. "A man would rather starve than beg", "A man who does not work hard is not a man", "Never let a girl pay for your meal" and so on. In the same way I exhort my children by saying: "The most important thing in life is to be humble and grateful", "Don't take anything for granted - don't be spoiled" and so on.

To encourage and comfort is a dad's special task. I cannot say for sure, but I really believe that the encouragement a dad gives is so important! Mom encourages the children all the time, always telling them that she loves them, often spontaneously several times a day. Dad does not encourage as often, and because of that his words sink deep into his children's hearts when he squats down, looks into their eyes and pours compliments over them. Dads, do not forget to encourage your children! It means so much, maybe more than you think! They need to know that you are proud of them. I will never forget when I was eleven years old and my dad looked deep into my eyes, and tear eyed and with a broken voice said that he was proud of me. What had I done? I had carried our dead dog three kilometers through the woods after it had been run over by the train, and then I buried it in our back yard. I even made a wooden cross and placed it in the ground. You may laugh at the story but I stood by that pile of dirt and cried when my dad came up to me, took me to the side and said "I am proud of you. Today you were a man." I still remember the feeling.

My dad's encouragement made me the man I am today. Men should be men and women should be women – that is the way it should be. That is how God has designed us. I am proud to be a man, husband and dad. I like being a man and I am not ashamed of the fact that I love hunting, fishing and professional boxing. The more I embrace my manhood, the more I can minister to my family. I love reading the Bible with my family and to provide for them; taking care of them is my greatest honor and joy in life.

SHE

The most beautiful description of the woman and her role as a wife is found in Proverbs 31:10-31 in the Old Testament. I encourage you to put this book aside for a moment and read that whole passage before you finish this chapter. Now, let us study how true Biblical femininity is defined:

> *A wife of noble character who can find? She is worth far more than rubies. Her husband has full confidence in her and lacks nothing of value. She brings him good, not harm, all the days of her life. She selects wool and flax, and works with eager hands. She is like the merchant ships, bringing her food from afar. She gets up while it is still night; she provides food for her family, and portions for her female servants.*
>
> **Proverbs 31:10-15**

1. Thought through, thinks about everyone and caring

Maybe it is a typical feminine attribute to be able to manage many things at once. This is a necessity for ordinary every day life to function. She shops for groceries while giving her daughter good advice on the phone. She cooks while helping her son with his homework. She cleans the house, does the laundry and folds it - all while watching the news on TV. Mom mows the lawn, cleans the pool and listens to an audio book, all at the same time. She remembers all the birthdays - even the cousins'. How does she do it? Well, she is a woman, plain and simple! She is a walking miracle! As a husband, dad and man I never stop being fascinated by Maria's ability to handle all these things simultaneously.

> *She considers a field and buys it; out of her earnings she plants a vineyard. She sets about her work vigorously; her arms are strong for her tasks. She sees that her trading is profitable, and her lamp does not go out at night. In her hand she holds the distaff, and grasps the spindle with her fingers.*
>
> **Proverbs 31:16-19**

2. Well planned and structured

It seems that the Bible considers it a feminine character trait to plan and be structured. I am sure it is, even though having an open and hospitable home is seen as a necessity for a wife and mom. There are however so many female administrators, secretaries and office managers in the business world and that is definitely not a coincidence. Generally speaking, the female sex is simply stronger in that area.

> *She opens her arms to the poor and extends her hands to the needy.*
>
> **Proverbs 31:20**

3. Good-hearted and thinks about the poor and needy

A woman has a softer heart than men do, and she usually wants to open up her home for the poor and needy. The desire to help needy people is a feminine attribute. There is something soft, warm, and empathetic in the female nature. God has placed this character trait in women in order to be able to take care of a baby and be a mom to toddlers. I know that some of my readers may get a bit upset now, but it is still a fact that men cannot breastfeed, and because of this does not have the same role during the first years of a child's life. Of course there are wonderful exceptions where a dad has become a widower, left alone to take care of a baby and things have worked out great. Likewise, there are success stories about single moms who have done a wonderful job raising teenage boys to become men. I am writing about the Biblical norm and what I believe is best for a child, but of course God gives grace for all sorts of unique situations.

When the snow comes, she has no fear for her household...

Proverbs 31:21a

She is clothed with strength and dignity; she can laugh at days to come.

Proverbs 31:25

4. Reliable and faithful

Another Biblical feminine attribute is reliability and faithfulness. Statistically men are more likely to commit adultery than women. Women are usually both more reliable and loyal in marriage and family life. It is a well-known fact that wives and mothers take their responsibility seriously by not letting the family down. Again, and sadly, there are exceptions where mothers have abandoned their marriages and children.

When Apostle Paul speaks about how they behaved as leaders in the church he said this:

... even though as apostles we could have asserted our authority. Instead, we were like young children among you. Just as a nursing mother cares for her children, so we cared for you. Because we loved you so much, we were delighted to share with you not only the gospel of God but our lives as well.

1 Thessalonians 2:6-8

The verses above speak about additional female attributes. The text defines what women are meant to be, and then especially a mother to her children.

It says that a mother cares for her children. She cares about her own children with a deep love. Many men have, like myself, married a girl whom we thought we knew, but a few years later she became a mother and changed drastically. The transformation from girl and young woman to mother was very clear and came almost like a shock, even though I personally thought it was a positive change. When my dear Maria became a mom I realized that this is what she was meant to be and created for. A woman flourishes in her femininity when she becomes a mom. That is why barrenness can be the greatest sorrow in a woman's life. Building a home, nursing children and pouring love upon them is deeply rooted in a woman. It is beautiful and it is very feminine. Personally I have thoroughly enjoyed watching my Maria be a mom. It comes so natural to her and she does it so well.

Men and women are different. Not only physically but also mentally (soul). We think, do, and prefer differently, and God's plan is for us to complement one another. We reflect God best together. Together we are invincible. That is how we reflect the Creator the most, since both male and female attributes are in Him. Let me just give you a few typical male and female things that will highlight our differences - and I am well aware that this will be a bit stereotypical and will not be completely true for all couples.

THE BIG AND THE SMALL

Men like to carry the new kitchen furniture from the truck to the kitchen but then let her decide exactly where the furniture should be placed and which tablecloth should go on the table. A man will buy 50 long stemmed red roses and goes all out while giving her the bouquet (preferably in front of an audience) accompanied by loud music. She would probably have preferred to receive one red rose every third day from him the whole year, but without the fanfare. He thinks large and grand while she thinks small and detailed.

I know it is stereotypical but I still believe it is rather striking. He wants to do something big for his family, like buying a vacation to Greece or getting a fishing boat - two or three BIG efforts for the family every year. He feels good. The project is complete! He can check it off the list. He is a good husband and father in his big (or small) head - whichever you want. She would probably prefer him spending every Saturday with her and the children, going on many small excursions instead of two BIG ones each year (even though she will not say no to Greece or a new boat). This is where conflicts tend to surface. He thinks she is never happy. To him it feels as though it doesn't matter how much time, money or energy he spends on the family - she always requires more. She thinks he is egotistical and selfish and not really present in the every day life. What really is going on is simply two people thinking very differently and they just need to learn how to meet in the middle. The big and the small are quite typical male and female attributes. If you just learn this you will find a much better harmony in your marriage and in your family.

WE REST DIFFERENTLY

Another typical male and female stumbling block is how you rest. When he rests he wants to do absolutely nothing, which is sleep, watch a movie, eat good food and then sleep some more. She wants to go on excursions and talk a lot since she has been alone with the children all day. He goes crazy and she goes completely haywire.

HONOR AND COZY FELLOWSHIP

He wants to be admired and she wants to be taken care of. He wants to hear: "You are so amazing, strong and funny!" She wants a blanket over her legs, a pillow under her head and a cup of hot tea while he runs his fingers through her hair, saying "you work so hard..." He is a trophy that is to be admired and shine in a place of honor, and she is a flower that is to be watered and spoken gently to. He needs honor and she needs cuddling. He needs respect and she needs much appreciation. We are different and because of that we also have very different needs.

> *However, each one of you also must love his wife as he loves himself, and the wife must respect her husband.*

Ephesians 5:33

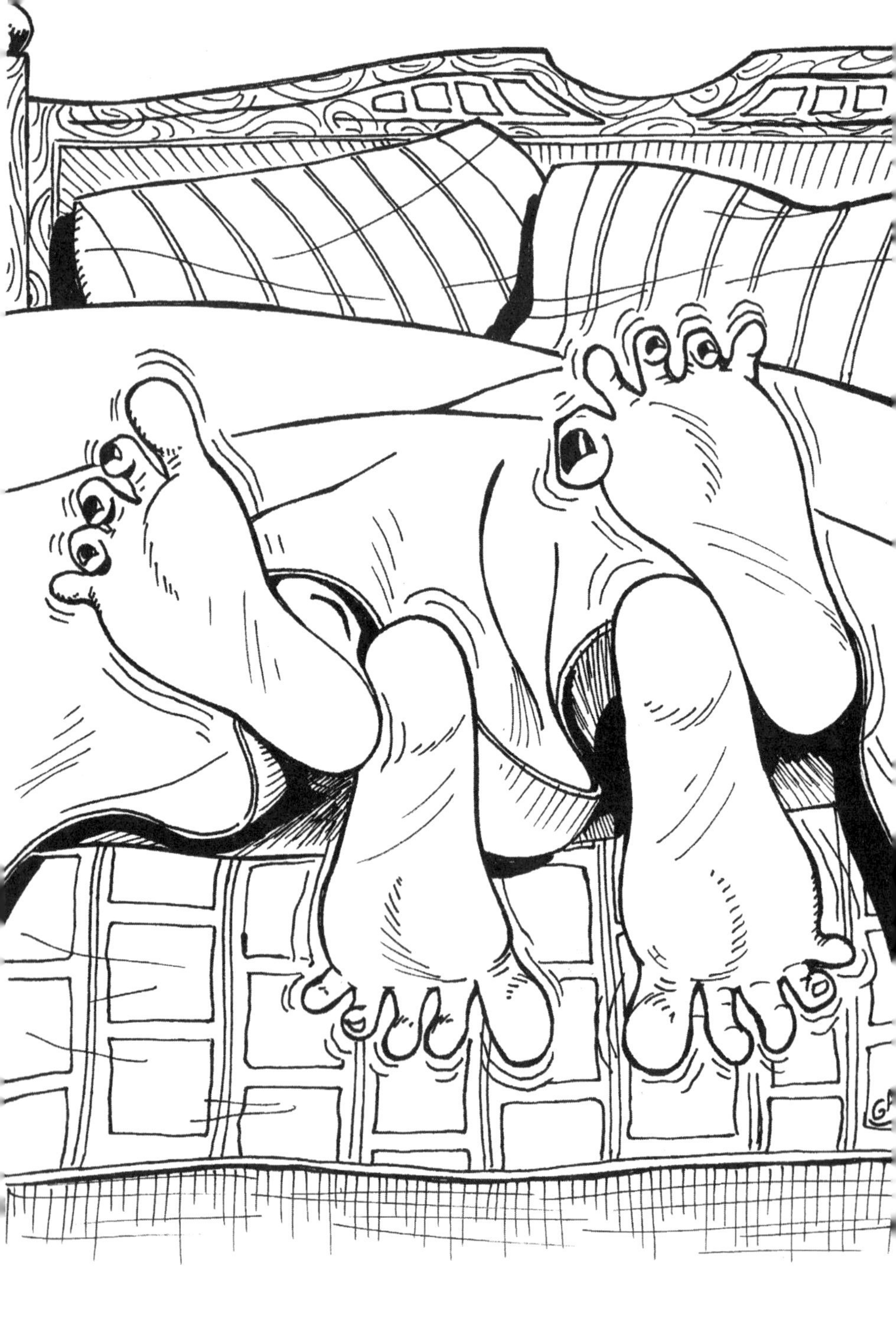

CHAPTER 6

SEX

But to Hannah he gave a double portion because he loved her...

1 Samuel 1:5a

Many books have been written on the subject that everybody sings about, longs for, and that so many seem to believe is the very meaning of life. Countless columns in magazines and newspapers all want to give you the best advice on how to have "a better sex life". Sex really isn't everything, but it should not be underestimated. Sex is as natural as it is beautiful, and is both an instinct and a need in almost every person's life. Sex unites two spouses intimately, but only if they at the same time work on having both spiritual and mental (soul) fellowship. If there is no unity in spirit and soul, sex will become shallow. If you are just focused on your own pleasure, soon enough it will only be all about different techniques, sexy lingerie and new experiments.

I will not even attempt to give you ten "new" ways to a better sex life in this book. Instead, I will try to shine light on what the Bible has to say about the topic. First of all, we need to understand that it is God who invented, created and came up with everything that has to do with married life. He who invented erection, orgasm and the g-spot will hardly blush at, nor is he prude or too holy to give guidance and advice.

God has created the attraction, the dynamics, the play and the interaction between man and woman. In the poetic Song of Solomon in the Old Testament, you will actually find astonishing and very frank verses about what the bride and groom say to and about one another.

The bride longs for the groom's deep kisses (Song of Solomon 1:2). Love is praised more than wine (1:4). The groom begins to describe his bride in detail, one body part at a time; cheeks, neck, eyes, hair, teeth, lips and mouth, feet and finally he almost goes crazy when he tries to describe her breasts! The groom almost seems to be high on testosterone when he moves on to describe her scent, taste and then slips over to describing her hips, belly button and breasts - again! He finally explodes and says with a trembling voice:

> *How beautiful you are and how pleasing, my love, with your delights! Your stature is like that of the palm, and your breasts like clusters of fruit. I said, "I will climb the palm tree; I will take hold of its fruit".*

May your breasts be like clusters of grapes on the vine, the fragrance of your breath like apples, and your mouth like the best wine.

Song of Solomon 7:6-9

What do you say to that? 3,000 years old Biblical love poetry, and you almost blush and wonder if what you just read was a forbidden erotic story on the Internet. Is this really the Bible? Yes, my friend, yes! The Bible celebrates sex between two spouses. The bride and the groom long to be united on the wedding night, and they compose the text freely and frankly. They long for one another, and they seem to do so with God's consent, or else it would not have been written in the Bible.

In the same love letter the bride describes the groom's eyes, cheeks, curls, hands and legs, and says that he is a piece of art, with a posture like the cedars! She describes her longing and says:

His left arm is under my head, and his right arm embraces me.

Song of Solomon 2:6

The reason why I show the frankness of the Bible when it comes to the bride's and groom's sexual desires and wild poems, is to de-dramatize. I want to say to all my readers that He who has created all of this is for it, and definitely not afraid to celebrate it. Sex is the Creator's gift to man and woman and there are no details written about what married couples may or may not do. Instead, the rule seems to be: As much cuddling, play and fantasy as possible in the bedroom! Surprise each other! And above all: dare to enjoy it and thank God for sex!

HE BELONGS TO HER AND SHE BELONGS TO HIM

Let me still be very clear on this: Sex belongs in a marriage. Only between two married spouses can sex be pure, celebrated and protected by the Creator. This is very clear in the Bible. Listen to what is says:

But if they cannot control themselves, they should marry, for it is better to marry than to burn with passion.

1 Corinthians 7:9

We are created to have sex, and God has deposited both the strong desire and the great need of closeness in us, and this can only be satisfied in one way. Because of this, the Bible is very practical in its advice to married spouses on the need and necessity of consistency in the sex life. The Bible's teaching is clear, and in the New Testament Apostle Pauls says:

The husband should fulfill his marital duty to his wife, and likewise the wife to her husband.

1 Corinthians 7:3

Spouses owe one another to satisfy each other sexually, which must mean that there has to be a mutual respect between the two. Both have a right to orgasms and variation. It should not just be one spouse who directs the activities in bed, but both must get to express what they long for and feel comfortable with. The boundaries are set together by the convictions of their hearts and consciences.

> *The wife does not have authority over her own body but yields it to her husband. In the same way, the husband does not have authority over his own body but yields it to his wife.*
>
> **1 Corinthians 7:4**

This passage is rather radical in today's society, but Paul simply underlines something that is very natural. You do not have the right to punish your partner by denying him/her sex, or to manipulate and use sex as a tool of power to get what you want. Many people do, and then they wonder why their spouse is no longer interested in having sex, or worse, is unfaithful. No, sex is a holy covenant act between two spouses and something that was given for us to stay together, not to create division. It should be self evident in a sound relationship that the husband gives his wife what she longs for and vice versa, and not always only thinks about himself. The one who gives the most receives the most. The one who serves and is perceptive to the partner's needs will reap greatly, even in the bedroom. The attitude should always be: "What do you want, honey? Tell me, so that I can make you happy!"

Do not deprive each other except perhaps my mutual consent and for a time, so that you may devote yourselves to prayer. Then come together again so that Satan will not tempt you because of your lack of self-control.

1 Corinthians 7:5

Paul goes on to say that long breaks in a consistent sex life is neither good for the marriage, nor when considering temptations such as unfaithfulness. Shorter breaks are ok from time to time, especially for those in spiritual leadership positions, but I think Paul is speaking about weeks, definitely not months.

Having sex at least twice a week is healthy between the ages of 25 and 50. Then it is quite natural for the frequency to drop a little since the sex drive begins to decrease. However, there are plenty of examples of couples who still enjoy each other sexually at a very old age. Enjoy the gift that God has given you while the flame of love is burning strongly.

WHEN YOUR WEDDING IS AROUND THE CORNER

If you are about to get married, maybe you should dial down your wedding night expectations just a tad. You will learn to have sex, practicing over and over again for 50 years, and eventually it will be really good. It may hurt and bleed the first time you have sexual intercourse, but it does not have to. It varies from couple to couple, and it may also depend on what kind of sanitary pad or tampon the woman has been using. Some girls who have used tampons for a long time will not bleed at all. Using birth control pills that may give you hormonal mood swings may not be the best way to start your life together. A better idea could be to wait for a while before you start trying to find the contraceptive that fits you the best, and just use condoms instead. I think you should ask your mom, mother-in-law or a nurse for advice. Throughout all time, experienced older women have given the younger women advice. Guys, talk to your dad, father-in-law, big brother or an experienced friend.

What contraceptive you end up choosing is not the most important thing, you will have a lot of fun and some really good times whatever you choose. In the beginning, avoid too advanced stuff and tricks in the bedroom, and let that come with experience instead. Remember that even if sex will improve technically over the years, it is really amazing just to be naked with your loved one on your wedding night. Sex is fun, amazing and beautiful. Sex is a gift from God to you! Once again, and in conclusion - enjoy the gift God has given you!

GAS

CHAPTER 7
THE CHRISTIAN HOME

But as for me and my household, we will serve the LORD.

Joshua 24:15b

Joshua, the great commander and general of the Jews in the Old Testament, said it so well in the verse above. The rest of you can do whatever you want, but me and my family will serve and follow God. Joshua decided to obstinately serve God, and everyone who lived under his roof had to come along whether they liked it or not. Nothing could change that!

The words household, home and family are used interchangeably in many parts of the Bible, and they all seem to mean the same thing. The Bible seems to speak more about some sort of big household than just "mom, dad, and children". Everyone who lived under the same roof was a part of the family - nuclear family, close relatives and even servants. The household that the father or the paternal head was responsible for could be between 2-30 people, and sometimes even more, depending on class and status.

THE HOME - AN EDEN

Our home is important, and the Christian home is supposed to be a stronghold and a refuge. God wants the best for us. If God had wanted us to suffer He would not have given the first two people on earth an Eden. God gave Adam and Eve a very beautiful garden in a tropical climate as a wedding gift. Their home was decorated, furnished and designed by God Himself. I like that thought. It reveals something about who He is and what He will for us is. Adam and Eve wandered in the garden, enjoyed life and relaxed in their first home. Their home was comfortable and extremely nice, to say the least.

> *Now the LORD has planted a garden in the east, in Eden; and there he put the man he had formed.*
>
> **Genesis 2:8**

Home is not a place we run from, but to. We want to be there as much as possible and every family member loves to be there. At home we can relax and really be ourselves. If that is not the case, it has to become that way. Eden means pleasure and exquisite happiness. We laugh the most and we are the happiest when we are at home. Your home should be your Eden.

THREE ACTIVE HOME BUILDERS

Unless the LORD builds the house, the builders labor in vain. Unless the LORD watches over the city, the guards stand watch in vain.

Psalm 127:1

A home does not just emerge out of nowhere, it must be built. A home has three active builders:

1. God
2. Husband
3. Wife

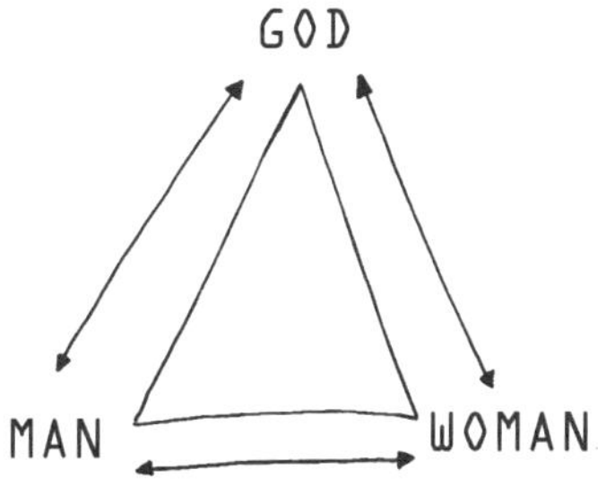

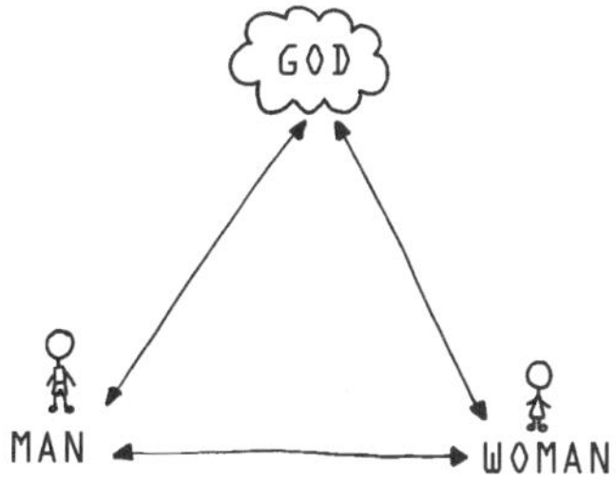

Invite God to build together with you! Some people hide behind the fact that God is building and do nothing themselves. Others have completely forgotten to put God into the equation. The first is over-spiritual nonsense and the latter is snobby shallowness. There needs to be cooperation where all three are active, contributing to building your home. God will build the house when the spouses humble themselves before Him and each other. A home that you all enjoy and where warmth, dignity and joy rule, is built in an atmosphere where God is feared.

A HOME SHOULD BE TIDY AND IN GOOD ORDER

I am not saying that a home always must be well cleaned and in some kind of meticulous order as a recipe for harmony. Happiness is not created just because you cannot find any dust in the corners or behind the sofa. The question you should ask yourself is this: What does your home look like in the spiritual realm? Is it clean? Does God thrive it in your place?

> *For the LORD your God moves about in your camp to protect you and to deliver your enemies to you. Your camp must be holy, so that he will not see among you anything indecent and turn away from you.*
>
> **Deuteronomy 23:14**

God moves about in a home where it is clean. God rescues and protects a family that is meticulous when it comes to asking one another for forgiveness and that does not keep too many secrets from each other. God enjoys living in a home where His Word is kept holy, is read and put to practice. God lives where prayer and worship is a lifestyle. He thrones on our worship and our gratitude. A strong spiritual atmosphere is created where humility and openness rule. When honesty and sincerity, but also laughter and warmth are around the family campfire, then God promises that He will move about in that camp. Great promise, right?

A HOME NEEDS BOTH A PRIEST AND A BOSS

For the husband is the head of the wife as Christ is the head of the church, his body, of which he is the Savior.

Ephesians 5:23

I am sure you already know that according to the Biblical order the husband is the head of the family. But, since the home is a woman's pride and sphere to some extent, there is actually a wonderful distribution of responsibilities. Let the husband be priest and the wife boss. The husband has the overall spiritual responsibility, and he reads the Bible with his family and is their first and foremost intercessor. She decides what groceries to buy, what is for dinner, what is planted in the yard, and she sets most of the rules for chores, laundry and cleaning. She is the boss and team leader with a right to veto and a great deal of power. Her word is law to the other family members. The family is the husband's primary responsibility, but the house is the wife's simply because then she can put her female touch on things. Of course it does not have to be like this, it can still work well if you are in agreement. This has worked out great for us, but you have to find your unique model through trial and error. Let me still highly emphasize that the husband carries the greatest responsibility for the family's well being in spirit, soul and body.

> *He must manage his own family well and see that his children obey him, and he must do so in a manner worthy of full respect. If anyone does not know how to manage his own family, how can he take care of God's church?*
>
> **1 Timothy 3:4-5**

The Bible is clear on the fact that the family is our greatest credibility. If you are a spiritual leader, you particularly need to understand that your family is the small church and the congregation is the big family. Family comes first. Every husband, dad and breadwinner of a family must understand that the family is the most important thing in his life, and it needs to be prioritized. He should not have other leadership responsibilities if his own family is nonfunctional, unhealthy and in disharmony. I love the fact that the Bible is so clear in its advice to husbands and wives regarding the family.

The Bible is so clear on how the family should be taken care of and prioritized, leaving no room for uncertainty in this matter. Family is our first and absolutely most holy calling. Apostle Paul even urges young widows by saying:

> *I counsel younger widows to marry, to have children, to manage their homes and to give the enemy no opportunity for slander.*
>
> **1 Timothy 5:14**

In other words, getting married, being a wife, giving birth to children and taking care of a home seems to be most important thing for every woman. Paul does not think that young women who have lost their husbands in war or accidents should waste any time. His simple advice and recommendation to young widows is: Get married again quickly, give birth to children, and build and take responsibility for a home.

WISE PLANNING

> *By wisdom a house is built, and through understanding it is established; through knowledge its rooms are filled with rare and beautiful treasures.*
>
> **Proverbs 24:3-4**

Building a family and home requires some strategic planning and regular family meetings. One way to do this is to have weekly planning meeting every Sunday night where the upcoming week's schedules are synchronized and tasks are delegated. Who will go to the PTA meeting at the boy's school on Monday night? Who will take the kids to horseback riding lessons and Tae Kwon Do on Tuesday and Thursday night? Who will go grocery shopping on Wednesday? Who will walk the dog on Friday afternoon before taking the teenager to youth service?

Building a happy, harmonious family requires its fair share of planning, however boring it may seem. Wisdom wins in the long run and it removes unnecessary tension and friction. Suddenly you will have time to sleep in on Saturday morning and then the whole family will sit around the table, playing cards, laughing together after a late brunch. Planning well eliminates unnecessary stress and creates space for a better quality of life. We actually had time to go to the gym together as a family and then go to a concert that same weekend without needing to compromise with church on Sunday. How did that happen? Planning ahead. The really important things need to be prioritized. We also need to learn to say no and remove certain activities in our lives that steal our focus and precious time. Your time is a gift from God. Time can contribute in building both marriage and family in an amazing way. Use and invest time wisely.

SAVE

A family must learn to set goals and save together. It brings the family together, and the vacation that you have been saving for will actually be even more enjoyable if everyone helps out. An emergency savings account for unexpected expenditures is also necessary to avoid a catastrophe if the car and fridge break down the same month. The goal is also to have some savings to give your children when they move out.

> *A good person leaves an inheritance for their children's children, but a sinner's wealth is stored up for the righteous.*
>
> **Proverbs 13:22**

The Bible goes as far as saying that we should even leave an inheritance for our grandchildren. Did you hear that? Remember that the unbelievers (the sinners) save for you without knowing it. When you walk in righteousness before God, their wealth is stored up just to be handed over to you one day, that is a promise from God. Start saving for your grandchildren and you will see what God will do for you. It is all about building a family with several generations in mind. Believe and pray for the coming generations and your inheritance will bless at least four generations down! You will not give them just a financial inheritance, but your children and grandchildren will inherit everything that you are and represent, if you believe that it is possible.

WHO IS YOUR SECRETARY?

Taking the overall responsibility is important for every husband, and it is one part of building a family. However, being the head of the family does not mean that you need to do everything by yourself. Your wife might be better at organizing the paperwork, doing math, the taxes, and understanding your bank's complex terminology, including its interest rates and mortgage language. Why not just drop your prestige and let her be the family secretary? Why hold on to something that you do not have the talent or ability to do? Who is best at paying the bills on time? The questions that you need to ask yourselves are: Who is better at what? Who is talented at what? You are meant to complement one another, not to compete. You are husband and wife. You are an invincible team as long as you stick together! Do not make fun of each other's flaws and weaknesses. Value each other. Do not hurt each other. Instead, cover, protect, and complete one another.

Mon — Dad pick up at preschool

Tue

Wed — Lisa soccer practice

Thu — PTO meeting at Josh's school

Fri — Grocery shopping

Sat — yard work
Basketball game

Sun

HOME SWEET HOME
Time Out Box
GAS

CHAPTER 8

RAISING CHILDREN

Children, obey your parents in the Lord, for this is right. "Honor your father and mother" - this is the first commandment with a promise: "so that it may be well with you and you may live long on the earth". And fathers, do not provoke your children to anger, but bring them up in the discipline and instruction of the Lord.

Ephesians 6:1-4

Children should obey their parents. According to the Bible that is just the way it should be. But it will not just happen - it is calling RAISING CHILDREN. Children need to learn to be subordinate to authorities and it begins with the parents. We are not being nice to our children by not raising them properly. On the contrary, your children will end up being disliked by both children and other adults if you are too nice and loose. No one appreciates a spoiled kid. Absolutely no one. And in the long run the children will not function together with other adults when the time has come for them to be a part of society, unless we teach them to face obstacles. Children need to face obstacles early in life and in an environment where they are loved and appreciated. Life is full of obstacles, miscalculations and disappointments, and it is our job as parents to teach our children how to handle this. It is our job as parents to create the best conditions for our children to succeed in their adult life. Our time is up when they move out, so take those years seriously. This is when you have your chance to really influence their future.

In the passage from Ephesians that we just read, Apostle Paul gives us three pieces of practical advice:

1. Do not provoke the children

2. Discipline the children

3. Instruct the children

If we provoke or tease our children, we will create distance between us, and a bad atmosphere at home. When parents tease their children, they undermine the close friendship that they want to have with them. Since children are both subordinate and dependent on their parents, teasing parents becomes a form of power abuse. Try not to provoke them, even if they sometimes do stupid, foolish, cute and funny things.

Fathers, do not provoke your children, or they may lose heart.

Colossians 3:21

To discipline means to train, teach and simply tell the children how things are done. They need to learn from someone how to function socially, verbally and practically - and this someone is you! Congratulations! You have just signed a 20-year employment contract! Your working conditions are as follows: Your salary and other benefits will not be disbursed until twenty years from now, you will have lousy working hours, attritional wear is to be expected, but at least your working colleague is good looking! You are your children's personal trainer, teacher, instructor and so on. If you do not teach your children how life should be lived, someone else for sure will, and they may teach them stuff you do neither want nor even stand for.

Do not withhold discipline from your children…

Proverbs 23:13a

To instruct is to explain in dialogue what is good and what is bad, all based on your own experiences. You will instruct your children more and more the older they get. Instruction will continue on through their teenage years, and hopefully also as they become adults. The goal is to build the kind of relationship with your children where they will come to you for advice even when they have grown up and left your home, right?

My son, if you accept my words and store up my commands within you, turning your ear to wisdom and applying your heart to understanding…

Proverbs 2:1-2

Listen, my sons, to a father's instruction; pay attention and gain understanding.

Proverbs 4:1

Since my children, Alicia and Adam, are only 15 and 13 years old, respectively, when this book is released, I do not want to give a bunch of advice and teaching from our own experience. I would rather wait a few years until we have crossed the finish line before I share our experiences. I pray that we will succeed! Maybe in time that will become a natural sequel to this book.

Instead I have chosen to share parts of an interview and conversation I had with Kurt and Annette Pettersson from Stockholm. They have been parents for more than 40 years and have managed to raise six biological children who all want to believe in, and follow Jesus as adults. All of their children, who have grown up and moved out, are doing great. They have also had two foster kids, and over the years, approximately 400 kids in need, have found a refuge in their home. They have very solid experience and lots of advice to give. Since they have lives that can back up every word they say on this topic, I will let Kurt and Annette give us some practical advice. Here is a condensed version of the Pettersson family's advice on raising children:

1. Why have you succeeded as parents, and why have your children done so well for themselves as adults? (Their answer is both humble and worth considering).

"We have said yes to God's calling to be a foster home, and this has released God's grace over our lives. Both our biological children and our foster children have come under God's special grace. All our children love God as adults."

My comment:

Their advice to us all is that when parents say yes to God's calling they will be happy and in harmony, and then their children will as well. A family has already succeeded when they live in the center of God's perfect will and most areas in their life will work out naturally.

2. What is the most important thing for a child to do well and be healthy?

"We believe all children need very clear rules and structures."

My comment:

According to Kurt and Annette, a sense of security is achieved when every family member is expected to follow the same rules. Children need to know when it is time to get up, when it is time to go to bed, and having their own chores will make them feel needed and included in the family. It is good for a nine year old to help clear the table, and an eleven year old can do the dishes, fill the dishwasher and mow the lawn. Twelve year olds can both clean and wash the car. Of course, they should start cleaning their own rooms at an early age. As teenagers they can do both the laundry, iron their clothes, and go grocery shopping. It is important that they learn that they do not live in a hotel, but that they are actually part of a family and are co-builders of a home.

3. What has been your strength and what have you done well together as parents?

"As parents we have always had the same opinion. The goal has been that the children should never be able to play one parent against the other. Same opinions and same rules have been our motto. "

My comment:

I went on to ask if they really had the same opinion all the time and always gave the same answers to the children. Annette answered that even when she did not agree with Kurt but the children had asked him first, and he had already answered, she chose to agree. She would tell the children that what dad had decided was correct, in order to neither create division nor confuse the kids, even if she had a different opinion. *"And then, when you are alone with your spouse, you can reason about it and agree upon what your common ground is"* says Annette.

Kurt has done the same. He always asked: *"What has mom said?"* and when they answered, he would say: *"Then that is what I say too"*.

4. What is most important for a child, apart from rules and structures, to be able to grow up and live a stable and harmonious adult life?

"All children, whether young or old, are in need of lots of love and care. When they are young they need to sit in your lap and be hugged. As they grow older they are still very dependent on love and care through words of affirmation and physical touch."

5. Are there times when spanking is okay when raising children?

"Through experience we have come to the conclusion that spanking never really did any good. We believe that you can actually raise children without spanking at all."

My comment:

Even though this is their firm belief today, the Peterssons humbly expressed that this was not their opinion from the beginning, but that as they and society morphed through the years, so did their stance and opinion. To make a point, there are times when you need to grab a hold of your children and let them know that it is not okay. If they are throwing a tantrum, you may need to hold them firmly until they calm down. *"But most of the time all Kurt needed to do was raise his voice,"* says Annette.

6. How do you discipline children effectively? What works and makes a difference when raising children?

"A disobedient child is most effectively disciplined by not letting them play with their favorite toy. Grounding a child works. Nowadays a confiscated cell phone, iPod or iPad is also very effective. Being consistent is important when disciplining children and not yielding when they nag about it halfway through. Stick to what you said. Do not discipline in anger, but think it through and make sure you agree with your partner, so that your words are not washed out and your children take you seriously."

7. It is common today for children to be diagnosed with ADHD or similar, and then have to live with it. Should a child with such a diagnosis or a handicap be treated differently?

"When it comes to children with such diagnoses it is important that the same rules apply to all the kids. Since it takes much longer for these kids to process information, you need to be very patient and understanding with them. But all children

should be treated the same. No children should be treated differently, even if they have such diagnoses or handicap. ADHD, Asberger's or being deaf in one or two ears makes no difference. The diagnose helps us adults to help the child appropriately and not treat him or her differently. A child that is treated differently due to a handicap diagnosis will feel excluded and like an outsider. The other siblings will also react negatively if the rules do not apply to all. This is a difficult question that can be faced from so many angles. We have had many children with different types of diagnoses that have lived with us over the years, and every child is unique, and has different needs."

I am so grateful that Kurt and Annette Pettersson were willing to share of their experiences and give some advice. Thank you!

GO TEAM!
GAS

CHAPTER 9

OUR GREATEST JOY!

I accidentally overheard a conversation (or an argument) between a husband and wife at an airport restaurant many years ago. I guess I was not supposed to hear, but they argued very loudly and unashamed at the table next to mine. Anyway, their fight inspired me to write this whole chapter, so I will leave it up to you to decide whether or not it was good that I eavesdropped.

The husband, who had obvious marital problems, sat there and quarreled with his wife. Red faced, sipping coffee, coughing and spitting crumbs, he kept repeating "Me, the kids and you." This phrase kept coming out of his mouth in various contexts, over and over again, just like a Hindu mantra. When I finally sat down in my airplane seat, all I heard was: "Me, the kids and you". This is what I heard: "Are we really gonna stay at that hotel, me, the kids and you?!" "Do you really expect me, the kids and you to drive around in this tiny tin-can rental car?!" And then with the most cynical voice: "ME, the kids and you at a concert? Well, won't that be sooo nice?"

He was outright tragic. He was an overgrown, spoiled and unbearable kid. He was a big bald child with stubble and a belly. He thought the kids and his wife were idiots and the most boring travel companions he could think of, not understanding what a pathetic loser he actually was. What if he would have just rearranged the words in his tragic mantra a little bit? What if he had said: "You, the kids and I" instead? What if he had cut the cynicism, the arrogance and the spoiled irritation, and actually taken his responsibility as a husband and father? How different everything would have been! "You, the kids and I! You first, honey. You were there before the kids and you will be there when we become empty nesters. Once it was just you and I and soon it will just be you and I again.

The kids are our most precious possession. The kids are our treasures and our greatest gifts! I come last, and my great joy, honor and task is to make you all happy. What a great vacation we will have! Where we stay does not really matter, and whatever car we squeeze into, we will still be the best family in the world. We build our own happiness and joy! Remember that joy is a choice and not just a vague feeling. We create our own happiness! Just imagine that we are going to a concert together! You, the kids and I, honey!"

RUN IN THE SAME DIRECTION

However, each one of you also must love his wife as he loves himself, and the wife must respect her husband.

Ephesians 5:33

Men have a great need for honor and respect. But to be honest how easy is it for a woman to show her husband honor and respect when he is being egocentric and really just another kid in their family? A husband who takes his responsibility is usually automatically honored. When a marriage is facing a crisis the husband is usually to blame. The Husband is strong and leading, for better and for worse. Because of that, men need to take their responsibility seriously, and above all else, take a close look at their own attitudes once in a while.

A man often thinks in terms of projects, and in his mind he keeps checking them off as they are reached. Then he moves on to new goals and new projects. A charming prince can turn into a pig shortly after the wedding ceremony since this is both a strength and a weakness. His project was to win her heart and carry her across the threshold, and now that he is done and she is conquered, he just drops everything. Being able to focus on working toward a specific target really is a man's strength. Until the prey is killed he is the persevering hunter, then he simply collapses of exhaustion.

Due to this, a man needs to be constantly challenged. The visions are the man's driving force. He builds a house. He gets a boat or a motorcycle and so on. A man needs to understand that a wife and children are not a project in the long line of projects.

They are not something that can be checked off on his mental list. No, they are his life. They are one with him. He needs to think "we" instead of "I". He needs to die to himself. The man needs to share his visions and plans with his wife so that they can set joint goals. They need to run in the same direction. They need to focus their energy on the same things. A mutual vision will build both marriage and family. Two visions will divide a family. Mutual projects will build both marriage and family. Separate projects will in the end create two different lives, and the spouses will grow apart. Think we instead of I.

Jesus says:

> *For this reason a man will leave his father and mother and be united to his wife, and the two will become one flesh. So they are no longer two , but one flesh. Therefore what God has joined together, let no one separate.*
>
> **Matthew 19:5-6**

Both husband and wife also need a healthy distance to their parents after the wedding ceremony. Not to the extent that they isolated themselves or break all contact with them, but they need to make it clear that they now have a stronger loyalty toward their partner. If the umbilical cord has not yet been cut, now is the time. The husband is not married to his mother, nor is the wife married to her father. It is us now. The priorities are: You, the children and I, honey. It is all about our greatest joy!

GAS

CHAPTER 10

TOO LATE FOR REGRETS

In the same way, husbands ought to love their wives as their own bodies. He who loves his wife loves himself.

Ephesians 5:28

A few years ago I came across a very interesting article based on a book written by the Australian nurse Bronnie Ware. The book is entitled "The Top Five Regrets of the Dying"*. The book is an interview-based study of people at the end of their lives. The book is a compilation of the astonishing results of talks between the author and patients in palliative care. The dying said:

1. I wish I had had the courage to live a life true to myself; not the life others expected of me.

This is what most people regret: postponing their dreams until there no longer was time to make them come true.

* 1. Ware, Bronnie. The Top Five Regrets of the Dying. USA: Hay house Inc, 2012. Print.

2. I wish I had not worked so hard.

Bronnie Ware writes that all the men, that are in their final phase of live, that she has cared for have all regretted spending so much time at work.

3. I wish I had had the courage to express my feelings.

4. I wish I had stayed in touch with my friends.

5. I wish that I had let myself be happier.

Did you notice that none of the top five regrets were "I wish I had worked out more?" Or "I wish I had bought more stuff." Nor did they say, "I wish I had been on more diets" or "I wish I had gotten divorced."

You are most likely reading this book due to one of the following three reasons:

1. You want to or are about to get married.

2. You are already married but seek advice on both raising your children and improving your marriage.

3. You face a marital problem or problems with your children and are in desperate need of help.

What these three categories have in common is that you still have the time and the possibility to change, to make decisions that will lead to a better life. One day it will be too late to regret the choices you have made. As long as there is life there is hope. You are alive. You are holding this book and have made it all the way to chapter ten. There is still hope!

Let us now go back to the top five regrets of the dying to make sure you will not do the same. Make a qualitative decision now! Say out loud that you will build the best family and marriage in the world! When turning eighty, you should not be found lying weeping in a bed in a nursing home.

Your last days should not be filled with anxiety and bitter, salty tears rolling down your cheeks. No! You should be able to look back on beautiful memories and be proud and pleased with how you have lived your life. You should be able to close your eyes and just feel peace and contentment. Let us just decide that that will be the case, okay?

CHOOSE LIFE!

Life happiness is actually a choice. Moses, the man of God said:

> *This day I call the heavens and the earth as witnesses against you that I have set before you life and death, blessings and curses.* ***Now choose life****, so that you and your children may live.*
>
> **Deuteronomy 30:19 (emphasis by the author)**

Choose life! Choose joy! Live the healthy, sound and positive life that you and your spouse have chosen together. Do not live a life dictated by others. What a liberation it was when Maria and I made the decision that we could care less what our neighbors thought. We are accountable to God and not to parents, relatives or friends. We live in the house we have chosen. We spend our time with friends that add and not drain. We do our own dream vacations and not someone else's. We tend to our yard as much or as little as we want, and we could not care less about what our neighbors think. We have a dog because we enjoy it, we work out, play cards and go to the movies. We dance to music in our living room, we laugh and embrace life. I hunt moose and Maria goes shopping when we have some free time. I go fishing and she does yard work.

Working less and spending more time with your family is something you will never regret. They will appreciate the time they had with you more than the extra cash or status that you can give them if you keep slaving away 50 or 60 hours a week. When I turned 40 I made a quality decision to work less. I sleep more than before and I eat healthier. I work out and take Tyson, our German Shepherd for long walks. Life definitely became radically different and so much better!

Tell your loved ones how much they mean to you and how much you love them! Do not wait until it is time to say goodbye before you say those well-chosen words. Say what you feel now since that opportunity may never come again. Stay in close contact with your mother, father and siblings. The hunting memories I have with my father are magical and totally unforgettable. All those moments at the camp fire in the woods with hot thermoses and dogs around our legs. The trip to Austria with all the siblings - I am so glad we actually did that! Take care of your loved ones. Go on fun and unforgettable vacations with your best friends! Do not just dream. Do not just think. Get your calendar out and start making plans. Put your plans into action, do it!

Allow yourself to be happy and have a good laugh, yes, laugh a lot, often and for a long time! Both my dad and grandpa were good at this and I am getting better and better. Sit down with your family and friends in the kitchen and just hang out. Spend time with each other in an undemanding, relaxed, and life-affirming way. Avoid wine and alcohol, which only destroys and creates problems and trouble.

Hang out in a safe and warm environment and dare to let go and loosen up. Enjoy life! Laugh from your belly with tears rolling down your cheeks.

One day we will look back at our lives and say "thank you God for my life! I am pleased! It has been amazing and now we will continue into eternity with singing, dancing and rejoicing!"

CLOSING WORDS

There is so much more to say about relationships, marriage, family and raising children. Like I always do when I write, I have just scratched the surface of this big subject. But I hope that I have been able to highlight something I believe most of us find very important. That is better than not doing anything at all, is it not? Dare to seek help when you need it. Do not wait until the catastrophe happens – take care of it sooner. Prevent the crises by living with a humble attitude towards advice and counseling. Checking the temperature of your marriage every now and then is sound. Every couple needs a marriage inspection at least once every five years. Remember that God is for you. Also remember that there are many warm and experienced couples out there who may have more marriage wisdom than you and who are a few steps ahead and would love to show you the way. How could seeking help ever be a defeat? Humility will guide your way to success

ABOUT THE AUTHOR

Johannes Amritzer preached his first message in 1991, and together with his wife Maria, he founded the mission organization Mission SOS in 1996. Initially SOS was a purely evangelistic ministry, but today it has become an apostolic ministry and home for hundreds of churches. In 2009 the Amritzers and a pioneer team planted SOS Church Stockholm. This is a church that, at the time this book is written, has over 60 nationalities represented and has become a spiritual home for people all over Stockholm.

Johannes is an evangelist who travels the world to preach the Gospel, particularly to those who have never heard it before. His passion and calling is to preach to Muslims, Hindus, Animists and Buddhists. Over the years, hundreds of thousands have given their lives to Jesus, and countless miracles have taken place in the over 70 Signs & Wonders Festivals that SOS has arranged so far. Over 600 churches have been planted, and today SOS also runs six international Bible schools where new church planters and missionaries graduate every year.

Today Johannes is the dad of SOS, overseeing the entire ministry, and he spends a lot of time coaching leaders and writing books. Books by Johannes Amritzer

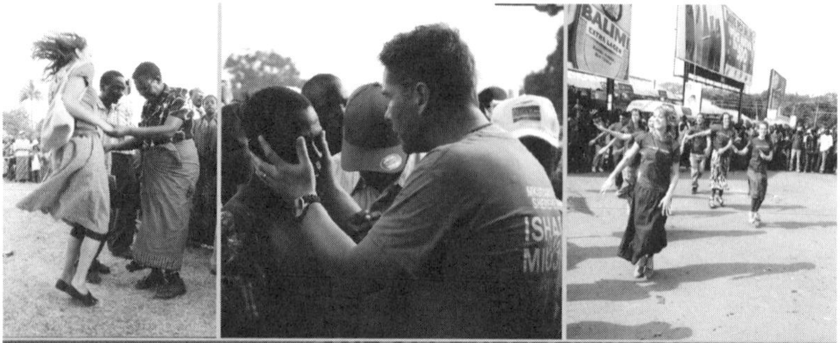